WINSOME PINNOCK

Winsome Pinnock's stage plays include *One Under* (Tricycle Theatre, and Graeae UK tour, 2019); *Leave Taking* (Liverpool Playhouse Theatre, National Theatre, Belgrade Theatre Coventry, Lyric Theatre Hammersmith and the Bush Theatre); *Una Calling* (Shakespeare's Globe); *Glutathione* (Young Vic); *The Principles of Cartography* (Bush Theatre); *Tituba* (Hampstead Theatre); *Cleaning Up* and *Taken* (for Clean Break at Ovalhouse Theatre); *IDP* (Tricycle Theatre); *The Stowaway* (play for young people, Plymouth Theatre); *Beg Borrow or Steal* (Kuumba Community Arts Centre); *Water* (Tricycle Theatre); *Talking in Tongues* (Royal Court Theatre Upstairs); *Mules* (Royal Court Theatre Upstairs and Clean Break Theatre); *Can You Keep a Secret?* (Connections at Royal National Theatre); *A Rock in Water* and *A Hero's Welcome* (Royal Court Theatre); *The Wind of Change* (Half Moon Theatre) and *Picture Palace* (Women's Theatre Group).

Radio plays include *Leave Taking, Madame Tempey, Singin' and Swingin' and Gettin' Merry Like Christmas* (adapted from Maya Angelou's autobiography), *Clean Trade, Her Father's Daughter, Let Them Call it Jazz* (adapted from a short story by Jean Rhys), *Indiana* (adapted from the novel by George Sand), *The Dinner Party, Something Borrowed, Water* (Radio 4) and *Lazarus* (Radio 3).

Rockets and Blue Lights received the 2018 Alfred Fagon Award. Other awards include the George Devine Award, Pearson Plays on Stage Award for best play of the year, and the Unity Theatre Trust Award. She received a special commendation from the Susan Smith Blackburn Prize. She was Senior Visiting Fellow at Cambridge University and writer-in-residence at Holloway Prison, Clean Break Theatre Company, Royal Court Theatre, Kuumba Arts Community Centre, Tricycle Theatre and the Royal National Theatre Studio. Her play *Leave Taking* received a major revival at the Bush Theatre in 2018 and a revival of *One Under* toured nationally and at the Arcola Theatre, London, by Graeae Theatre Company in autumn 2019.

Other Titles in this Series

Winsome Pinnock

ROCKETS AND BLUE LIGHTS

NICK HERN BOOKS

London

www.nickhernbooks.co.uk

A Nick Hern Book

Rockets and Blue Lights first published as a paperback original in Great Britain in 2020 by Nick Hern Books Limited, The Glasshouse, 49a Goldhawk Road, London W12 8QP

Rockets and Blue Lights copyright © 2020 Winsome Pinnock
Lyrics copyright © 2020 Femi Temowo

Winsome Pinnock has asserted her right to be identified as the author of this work

Cover photography by Lee Baxter

Designed and typeset by Nick Hern Books, London
Printed in Great Britain by Mimeo Ltd, Huntingdon, Cambridgeshire PE29 6XX

A CIP catalogue record for this book is available from the British Library

ISBN   978 1 84842 940 6

Rockets and Blue Lights was first performed at the Royal Exchange Theatre, Manchester, on 13 March 2020. The cast was as follows:

BILLIE	Anthony Aje
TURNER/ROY/PETER PIPER	Paul Bradley
THOMAS/TREVOR	Karl Collins
LOU/OLU	Kiza Deen
CAESAR/REUBEN	Natey Jones
ESSIE/LUCY	Rochelle Rose
RUSKIN/JOHNSON/DECKER	Matthew Seadon-Young
JESS/JEANIE	Kudzai Sitima
DANBY/MARY/MEG/VONNIE	Cathy Tyson
CLARKE/PEARSON/BENJAMIN	Everal A. Walsh

Director	Miranda Cromwell
Designer	Laura Hopkins
Lighting Designer	Jessica Hung Han Yun
Sound Designer	Elena Peña
Composer/Musical Director	Femi Temowo
Associate Musical Director	Elizabeth Westcott
Associate Director	Mumba Dodwell
Assistant Director	Chantelle Walker
Voice/Dialect Coach	Joel Trill
Casting Director	Vicky Richardson CDG
Stage Manager	Louise Martin
Deputy Stage Manager	Sylvia Darkwa-Ohemeng
Assistant Stage Manager	Sarah Barnes
Rehearsal Historian Consultant	Dr Gemma Romain
Rehearsal Historian Consultant	Dr Kristy Warren

With special thanks to Barbara Crossley and Martyn & Valerie Torevell for supporting the creation of this production.

For Vivia, Ayana, Gifford, Affoline and Steve

Characters

2006/2007

LOU, *an actress, black, plays Olu in* The Ghost Ship
REUBEN, *African-American marine archaeologist*
TREVOR KING, *forties, a writer/director, black*
ESSIE, *thirties, a teacher, black*
ROY, *mid-sixties, an actor, white, plays Turner in*
  The Ghost Ship
BILLIE, *twelve years old, black*
VONNIE, *Lou's sister, black*
CLARKE, *eighties, Lou's grandfather, black*
ACTOR PLAYING PEARSON
ACTOR PLAYING JOHNSON

1840

THOMAS, *a sailor, black*
LUCY, *his wife, black*
JESS, *fourteen/fifteen, their daughter, black*
MEG, *seventies, a runaway, black*
J.M.W. TURNER, *artist, white*
BILLIE, *twelve years old, black*
BENJAMIN, *a beggar, black*
PETER PIPER, *a beggar, a blacked-up white man*
HANNAH DANBY, *Turner's housekeeper, white*
MARY, *Turner's mother, white*
DECKER, *a recruiting officer, white*
CAESAR, *a shantyman, black*
RUSKIN, *artist, white*

Suggested Doubling

ESSIE/LUCY
LOU/OLU
THOMAS/TREVOR
REUBEN/CAESAR
CLARKE/PEARSON/BENJAMIN
TURNER/ROY/PETER PIPER
RUSKIN/JOHNSON/DECKER
DANBY/MARY/MEG/VONNIE
BILLIE
JESS

Note on Play

Two of the many inspirations for this play are J.M.W. Turner's paintings: *The Slave Ship* (*Slavers Throwing Overboard the Dead and the Dying – Typhoon Coming On*) and *Rockets and Blue Lights*. Popular belief is that *Slavers* portrays the *Zong* massacre which took place when Turner was a child, but some think it tells another story. Either way the painting suggests the ongoing legacy of the slave trade. The play explores this legacy and attempts to reconstruct the lives of black Londoners after abolition. The slave trade ended in 1807, but slavery wasn't properly abolished until around 1838, and may have continued beyond that.

This text went to press before the end of rehearsals and so may differ slightly from the play as performed.

Prologue

2007. ESSIE *and* LOU *stare at Turner's painting* The Slave Ship (*which the audience can't see*) *on the 'fourth wall' of a museum on board a ship, which is the reproduction of a slaver.* LOU *wears a beautiful designer gown and jewellery.*

LOU *glances at* ESSIE *who is absorbed in the painting.*

LOU. Tell me what you see.

ESSIE. The ship tries to distance itself from the nightmare, but is dragged back to the furious feeding frenzy by the undertow. Amber, gold, chrome, the darkest darkest sea.

LOU. I nearly drowned once. At the lido in Streatham. Swimming bodies made it look easy, so I dove in. When they fished me out I was limp, dead for a split second. Why does he make something so ugly beautiful?

ESSIE. Other painters produce noble victims or make the abolitionists into saints; Turner comes up with this portrait of a massacre. It's incredible. (*Slight pause.*) What do you see?

LOU. A pair of disembodied black tits, and a leg that looks like a pig's trotter.

They both laugh.

They gaze at the picture.

ESSIE. At first you can't make out what's going on. You have to look, really look. You can't turn away.

Slight pause.

LOU. When I look at this painting I think about his amazing use of colour, his elegant suggestion of bloodshed in a captured sunset. The only person we can see has her head submerged in the water. I look at this painting and I don't think about what's just happened to those poor men, women, children. They're invisible.

ESSIE. We can't see the drowning bodies but we know they're there. We have to imagine, and what we imagine is so much worse than anything he could show us. He turns the world upside down. The sky reflects the carnage underneath. You can taste the blood in the water, you can hear their screams.

LOU. And we just stand here looking; watch their hands search for ours, knowing full well that we can't help them.

ESSIE. The critics bludgeoned him for this. They all thought he'd gone mad.

Silence. ESSIE *takes a sneaky sidelong look at* LOU *as she contemplates the painting.*

LOU. When I look at this I feel as though I'm inside Turner's mind. And that is not a good place to be.

ESSIE. It's art. All it can do is bear witness.

They look at the painting. LOU *takes a quick sidelong look at* ESSIE.

LOU. I'm getting together with a few friends later. There'll be a lot of creative people there. I think you'll find it interesting. Will you come?

ESSIE. I er… I um… thank you, but I –

LOU. You've heard of Reuben Sumner?

ESSIE. Of course… he's amazing. He makes those underwater sculptures…

LOU. He's also – you know, for his day job he's a marine archaeologist. He was historical adviser on that film about Turner.

ESSIE. Oh yes, that film. *The Ghost Ship.*

LOU. Have you seen it?

ESSIE. Yes, I've seen it. It has its moments, but…

LOU. I know what you mean. England is an abolition theme park right now, and I hate the way this painting contributes to the abolitionist narrative of white saviourism.

ESSIE. Does it, though? I mean look at it, it's an extraordinary indictment of those very narratives, isn't it?

BILLIE *enters carrying a clipboard.*

Hello, you. What are you doing here? Where's Mr Richmond?

BILLIE. Don't know, miss.

ESSIE. You're supposed to be doing the Coffle Walk with him.

BILLIE. I don't like him, miss. I prefer to hang with you.

ESSIE. Just because we're not on school property doesn't mean that we're 'hanging out'. You've got to treat today like one long lesson.

BILLIE (*notices* LOU). Oh my days. It's her. Captain Thingy. It's her, miss.

ESSIE (*amused by* BILLIE*'s excitement*). What are you talking about?

BILLIE. It's her, miss. Off the telly. Captain Sola Andrews of the space ship *SS Rego.*

ESSIE. Oh. (*Suddenly realising who* LOU *is.*) Oh.

BILLIE. What's she doing here, miss?

LOU (*holds her hand out*). Very nice to meet you.

BILLIE *and* ESSIE *are star-struck, stand with their mouths open.* ESSIE *quickly pulls herself together.*

ESSIE. Where are your manners, Bille? Say hello.

LOU *shakes* BILLIE*'s hand. He can hardly speak.*

BILLIE. And she's in that film. I seen the posters everywhere. Can I have your autograph, Captain?

LOU. Of course. And you don't have to call me Captain. You can call me Lou. Do you have a pen? Where shall I sign?

BILLIE *gives* LOU *his clipboard.* LOU *looks at it.*

You're a very talented artist.

BILLIE. It's this boat-museum, Captain.

LOU (*to* BILLIE). I don't want to sign on that, do I? It'll look as though it's my drawing instead of yours. (*Turns the page, signs.*) There.

BILLIE. It's going to take us up the river. When's it sailing, miss?

ESSIE. It's leaving at five o'clock, after the Coffle Walk.

BILLIE. Are you coming with us?

LOU. Me? Oh no. I've just come to look at this painting.

LOU *hands back the clipboard.*

I'll tell you a secret, though: This is the boat we used in our film.

BILLIE. Is it? Wow.

LOU. The production company donated it to the Foundation and they turned it into this floating museum.

BILLIE. And I'll tell you a secret... I'm going to be famous, too. I'm going to be a footballer or a boxer, or a street dancer.

LOU. Well, you've got a lot of options there.

BILLIE. Man U's gonna buy me for millions of pounds.

ESSIE. Run off and find Mr Richmond, Billie. He'll be going mad with worry.

BILLIE. Do I have to, miss?

ESSIE. Yes, you do. Go on. I'll catch you up.

BILLIE. I think you're awesome.

LOU. Well, I think you're awesome too.

BILLIE *is made up. He runs off.*

ESSIE. I'm sorry... I didn't... I didn't recognise you...

LOU. I wouldn't have got talking to you if you had.

ESSIE. You've been nominated for an award, haven't you? Of course. That's why you're... I love your dress. Aren't you going to be late?

LOU. I'm not going. No point. I won't win.

ESSIE. You might. It's an interesting film.

LOU (*suddenly*). Did you see that? The woman in the painting. She moved.

ESSIE. Sorry?

LOU (*laughs at herself*). I thought I saw… That's ridiculous. There! Look, she did it again. She pulled her head out of the water. She looked right at me. Jesus, it's time for me to leave. I've got to get ready for the… You are coming, aren't you?

ESSIE. If you're sure…

LOU. Here's the address. (*She gives* ESSIE *her card.*) You know, when Turner died John Ruskin tried to burn his old friend's secrets: lurid sketches he'd discovered of genitalia and couples fucking. To my mind that proves Turner's pornographic tendency. I'm not surprised that this painting drove Ruskin mad. It's beginning to have the same effect on me.

ACT ONE

Scene One

2006. London. A rehearsal room. TREVOR *is on his mobile phone.* REUBEN *is putting papers into files. The actors playing* PEARSON *and* JOHNSON *sit together, going over lines.* JEANIE, *the PA, has a tape measure around her neck and is handing out cups of tea and coffee.*

ROY. Fancy meeting you here. Long time no see.

LOU. Good to see you, Roy.

ROY. Me and Deanne were talking about you just the other day.

LOU. How is Deanne?

ROY. You know Deanne. You changed your number? I tried calling a couple of times, couldn't get through.

LOU. I'm mostly based in the States now, Roy.

ROY. Yes, I heard.

JOHNSON. 'She danced?'

PEARSON. 'I made sure of that'. Sorry-sorry. (*Tries the line again with different intonation.*) 'I made sure of that.'

ROY. You excited? It's ages since I done a film.

LOU. Did Trevor just say that there were rewrites?

ROY. They're very good. Didn't you get them?

LOU. I've just got off a plane. Jeanie's just printed me a copy.

ROY. You just got off a plane?

JEANIE (*to* LOU). While I've got you, can I take your measurements?

ROY. Jack of all trades today, you.

JEANIE (*taking* LOU*'s measurements*). The designer's caught the lurgy.

ROY. Just popping out for a fag.

ROY *goes*.

REUBEN. I'm Reuben. We spoke on the phone.

LOU. Yes-yes. I looked up your work. Your sculptures are amazing.

REUBEN. I'm honoured that you… I'm a great admirer of your work, Miss Clarke.

LOU. Please call me Lou.

REUBEN. I put together some research for you – articles, images you might find interesting. It'll save you having to read all the books.

REUBEN *hands* LOU *a folder.*

LOU. Thank you. That's helpful.

ROY. Where's mine, then? Don't I get one of those?

REUBEN. Sorry-sorry. I only made one copy.

ROY (*winks at* LOU). Of course you did.

TREVOR. If you're all ready shall we make a start? Everyone take a seat, please. Roy, where's Roy?

ROY. All present and correct.

REUBEN. The thing is history only tells you so much. The real stories are lost in time. But if you do want book recommendations just let me know. Anything you need, anything at all I'm right here.

LOU. That's very kind. I do have a question: how do you decide where in the ocean you're going to put your sculptures?

REUBEN. I can't give away all my secrets, can I?

LOU. Spoilsport.

TREVOR. Jeanie, can you tell everyone we're starting and round up the others.

The others find their seats. Actor playing PEARSON *seems oblivious, trying different ways to say his lines.*

PEARSON. *I* made sure of that. I made *sure* of that. I made sure of *that*.

TREVOR. Jeanie, will you read the directions?

JEANIE. Me? But I'm supposed to be... all right. If you want me to. Okay.

JEANIE *moves her seat.*

TREVOR. When you're ready.

JEANIE (*reading*). *The Ghost Ship* by Trevor King. Scene One. Exterior, the Atlantic Ocean. 1781. It is the middle of the night. The ocean so tranquil that we cannot distinguish between sea and sky. Gulls flap languidly across a purple sky studded with stars. A solitary dolphin plummets underwater. In these deeper waters the creature moves into the dappled light from the moon and is at once surrounded by floating objects. It is a sublime and magical moment, until we realise that these objects are severed limbs: a hand, a foot, a torso; a head whose visage is twisted into a grimace of pain. A whole body plunges into the water, writhing in slow motion as though in space. It is a child. We see him struggle with the water, trying to swim back to the surface, but the effort is futile as he succumbs to the power of the current. The dolphin surfaces and the silence of the deep sea explodes into the screaming chaos of a massacre. We see the impressive tall ship in silhouette, its sails at full mast and sailors on deck dragging struggling and enchained Africans then throwing them overboard. Interior, the ship's hold. Night. Olu, chained to two other women, listens to the carnage taking place on deck, amidst the screaming and fear of the women below. Suddenly, the hold is lit with the light from a burning torch shone into it by sailors who descend and grab more women, dragging them to the hell above. One of the sailors, James Pearson, approaches Olu. He unlocks her chains so that she is separated from the other women. He grabs her by the waist. She struggles, kicking and biting. He lashes her and ties her chains around her and throws her across his shoulder. On the deck he hoists her over the side of the ship. She clings on to the rigging. Beneath her the sea boils with the excited sharks below. She grabs hold of the sailor's arm. Although he does not speak her language, he understands that she is pleading with him to save her life. He gives in and starts to haul her up. Behind him the thunderous commands of his captain. He lets her go... She gasps but doesn't have time to scream before she disappears into the sea, obscured by the froth of thrashing sharks. (*Slight pause.*) Cut to Interior, Night. 1840. Turner's studio. Turner, gin bottle in hand, contemplates an empty canvas...

Pause. They look at ROY *who has the next line.*

LOU. Roy? Roy?

ROY. It's me. I know. I just... Bloody hell, man. Bloody hell.

Scene Two

1840. Turner's studio. Night. TURNER *and* DANBY *having sex.* LOU*'s face appears in the window, watching them.* TURNER *sees her. She smiles and waves. He loses focus for a moment, but he repositions himself, turns his back to her and gets on with the job. After the sex* TURNER *tidies himself. He walks to the window and checks it. There's no one there.* DANBY *buttons herself up.*

TURNER. Pack me a bag, Danby. I'm off.

DANBY. Is that it? No kind words, no thank you?

TURNER. You should thank me. That's pedigree blow up yer, that is.

DANBY. Charming.

TURNER. The blow of a genius. What more do you want?

DANBY. Constable wouldn't talk to his woman like that.

TURNER. Cunt-stable never had a woman. He had a wife.
He was a gentleman – (*Self-mocking*.) I am an artist.

DANBY. You shouldn't speak ill of the dead.

TURNER. That's what they say about his paintings.

TURNER *groans and holds his jaw in pain*.

DANBY. Tooth still at you? That's divine retribution, that is.
Come here.

TURNER *opens his mouth*. DANBY *takes a small vial
of peppermint oil out of a pocket and pours a drop onto
the tooth*.

TURNER. A cab, Danby.

DANBY. Where shall I say you're going?

TURNER. I'll tell 'em when they get there.

DANBY. You said you was going to paint me. You said that
I have the face of the goddess Scylla and that I should be
immortalised in paint.

TURNER. There is an uncanny likeness: Scylla was a monster
with six heads.

DANBY. Think you're so funny, don't you?

TURNER. You want me to paint yer?

DANBY. Yes, Mr Turner. Turn me into a goddess.

TURNER *squeezes paint out of a tube onto his hands and
smears her face with paint*.

TURNER. Done.

DANBY. You old rantallion. I don't have to put up with this
constant humiliation. I'm leaving. I mean it. Do you think
I enjoy cooking and cleaning for yer, mixing those bloody
pigments? Look what they've done to my face.

TURNER. Stop your hollering. You want all the street to know
my business?

DANBY. I mean it this time. Find yourself some other fool.

TURNER. You're leaving are you? And where you going,
Danby? Eh? Who else'd have you?

DANBY. There's plenty would take me in.

TURNER. Look at the state of you. You belong here with me.
Two ugly little orphans together. We're like brother and
sister, you and me; mother and son.

DANBY. You're old enough to be my grandfather. And who
you calling ugly? Why shouldn't I be the subject of a
painting? And I'm not talking about being no onlooker either
while them's think they're better than me get the centre of
the canvas. Problem is I'm too beautiful. That's what it is,
isn't it, my beauty blinds you.

TURNER. Shush. Shush. Calm now, Danby, calm. Thas it. You
want me to paint you I'll paint you. Sit. I shall paint you as
both Scylla and Charybdis.

*She sits. He stands in front of a canvas and picks up a brush
and palette, stares at her as if waiting for her to do something.*

Acting like you ain't never sat for an artist before. The pussy.

DANBY *sighs – here we go again.*

Show me. Open it.

She opens her legs wider.

With your fingers. I want to see inside you.

*She follows his instructions. He bends to look inside her, then
inserts a finger. He pulls it out and smells it.*

You smell of the sea. (*He smears her juices across the
canvas then sucks his fingers.*) Taste like it too.

DANBY. And what do you taste of?

TURNER. Eh?

DANBY. I'll paint you, shall I?

DANBY *gets up from her pose.*

TURNER. Behave yourself, Danby.

DANBY. Open it. I want to see inside you.

DANBY reaches into TURNER's trousers from behind and masturbates him.

Not so arrogant now, eh, Turner? Your patrons don't see this when they contemplate your brilliance, do they? They imagine a celestial outpouring, not this dirty vigorous hand.

TURNER escapes from DANBY.

TURNER. Get the cab.

DANBY. Where you off to this time?

TURNER. Wouldn't you like to know?

As they speak, TURNER puts his coat on. DANBY helps him. She knows the form and pins his sleeve to the front of the coat to make it look as though he only has one arm.

DANBY. I would as it happens. You're always off.

TURNER. Constable was right about one thing. Painting is more science than art. I have experiments to undertake.

DANBY. What am I to tell your friends when they come a calling?

TURNER. Tell them to keep their noses outta my business. London's too many distractions.

DANBY. Am I to come with you?

TURNER. Have I ever brung you with me on my travels?

DANBY. I could carry your knapsack. I've always wanted to go to Rome.

TURNER. Who says I'm off to Rome? You're to look after the gallery, make sure my darling children are protected from sun and rain.

DANBY. And what if Sarah comes and enquires about your flesh-and-blood children? What shall I tell her?

TURNER. She'll see me when I return. How do I look?

DANBY. I don't know why you bother with disguises. The men at sea don't know who you are. Don't go. Don't leave me all on me own again.

TURNER. You've got the paintings, haven't you? What more do you want?

DANBY. There is that. And I do like to sit and look at them. When will you be back?

TURNER. When I'm back. Now, go and get that cab.

DANBY *goes*. TURNER *returns the umbrella to its sheath, gets himself together. Tucks his shirt in, etc*. MARY *appears at the window, she opens it*.

MARY. Running away to sea again, are yer? Running away from the truth?

TURNER. Is that you, Danby? Having a little joke with me? Very funny. Enough now.

MARY. Go on then, run away. You know as well as I do that it'll just follow you wherever you go.

TURNER. Shut up and go away. You don't exist. You're dead. I've got a death certificate to prove it.

MARY. Maybe you're mad too. That's what they're all saying at the Academy: 'Turner's taken a turn. Just like his mum.' A mother might expect a son to defend her, not stuff her away to languish in Bedlam for the rest of her days. No boy can treat his mother that way and get away with it. I was the one who'd take you down to the beach, dip your little toesies in the foam. I was the one gave you your muse. It's my memories in your brain guiding your paintbrush. What thanks do I get for it? Tried to silence me, afraid of what secrets I'll spill. Who do you think you are, Joseph Mallord William Turner? You're not so old that I can't smack your pompous arse. Whatever you think of me, I will always be your mother and that means something.

TURNER. Fuck off and haunt someone else, you mad old bitch.

TURNER *leaves*.

Scene Three

1840. The docks. The presence of a ship, The Glory, *is suggested.* TURNER *is sketching the ship.* THOMAS, *a sailor, enters.* BILLIE *plays upstage.*

THOMAS. You waiting on the recruiting officer for *The Glory*?

TURNER. Aye.

THOMAS. Met him yesterday in The Royal Oak. Told me to come back and sign ship's articles. He say that to you?

TURNER. I ain't met him yet.

THOMAS. I'll wait with yer, if you don't mind. He will come, won't he?

TURNER. I've never known a crimper forgo blood money.

THOMAS. I ain't been crimped. I'm signing them articles of my own free will. You?

TURNER. If they'll have me.

   THOMAS *sits on the ground and takes out a handkerchief. Unfolds it to reveal a hunk of bread. He offers some to* TURNER *who shakes his head.* THOMAS *eats.* TURNER *continues sketching.*

THOMAS. We'll look out for each other. One more voyage then I'll settle down.

TURNER. The sea's a difficult mistress to forsake.

THOMAS. Tell me about it: She won't let me go. God knows I've tried. I've a wife of flesh and blood, but there's no comparison. My wife has a tempestuous jealousy.

TURNER. But she don't mind you going?

THOMAS. She don't know I'm here. You have a wife?

TURNER. Not right now, no.

THOMAS. Then you're a lucky man. You've no one to answer to. I love the sea, its power. Don't you love just to look at it? The way its emotions change from moment to moment. This sea has swallowed ancient worlds alive, and one day she'll belch them out again. Belch out all her secrets – (*Referring to* The Glory.) magnificent ship, isn't she?

TURNER. Old girl now.

THOMAS. She's life in her yet. She's good for a few more voyages. (*Slight pause as he looks at* TURNER. *Holds his hand out.*) Thomas.

BILLIE *approaches. He is wearing chains.*

BILLIE. Mister, have you got the key?

THOMAS. What you doing with yourself, you little mudlark?

BILLIE. Fished them out of the water.

THOMAS. They're not baubles. Take 'em off.

BILLIE. I can't. I'm stuck.

THOMAS. You'll have to ask 'em over there. I ain't got no keys.

BILLIE *cries.*

BILLIE. Please, mister. Get us out. It hurts. I'll be like this forever now.

THOMAS. Over there I said. They've got the keys to free you.

BILLIE *runs inside.*

Little urchin. (*To* TURNER.) What's your name, then?

TURNER. Booth.

THOMAS. I can tell by your blistered hand that you are a man of the sea.

TURNER (*proud*). Grafted all my life, I'll grant you that.

CAESAR *enters and waits.* THOMAS *looks at* TURNER*'s sketch.*

THOMAS. You've done her proud. The perfect arc of her like a full-bodied woman. Teak from Burma, mahogany from the Honduras. Lined with steel, she is. She'll go steady in the toughest storm. That prow will cut through the sea like a knife through dripping. Here he is.

DECKER, *the recruiting officer, enters.*

DECKER. What we got here, then? Come along quick. I ain't
got all day. Tell me your names and the post you hold.

CAESAR. Caesar. Able seaman and shantyman.

DECKER. A musician? Let's hear a song, then.

CAESAR *sings a sea shanty.*

CAESAR. Watch the wind as she blows
Our sails as she flows
Working another day
And I in the middle, seeing them play
Working another day

See the waves as they're crashing
Our wooden queen thrashing
Working another day
And I in the middle, seeing them play
Working another day

DECKER. Nice. A little melancholy, though. You know any
happier songs?

CAESAR *starts to sing again.*

Not now. Save it for the voyage. I'll have articles for you.
We sail tomorrow afternoon.

CAESAR. Thank you, sir.

DECKER. And you?

THOMAS. Ship's cook. They tell me I've the magic touch.
Once, when the rations was all spoiled I roasted the rats
responsible for the spoliation and nobody knew the
difference, licked their fingers and asked for more.

DECKER. You're making me mouth water just thinking about
it. You're in. Any more for any more?

TURNER. What about me?

DECKER. We've got enough old men for one voyage. And
we've definitely no use for half an elderly man.

TURNER. I lost my arm in Trafalgar. That must count for something. I fought for you young blighters and you have the bloody cheek to / dismiss me

THOMAS. He may only have one arm, but that one arm is full of gifts. He is a ship's artist. His art will give the crew something more to contemplate than their own carnal desires. Music and art will ensure a smooth journey.

DECKER. Ship's artist, eh?

THOMAS. He'll paint your likeness.

TURNER. What?

DECKER. I've always wanted to be painted.

THOMAS (*sotto voce*). Show him the sketches.

THOMAS *takes the sketches and shows them to* DECKER.

DECKER. And you'll paint me?

TURNER. If you like, yes.

DECKER. It's against my better judgement, but you're in. I can't stand about looking at art all day. I've got to drag the captain off his betrothed and get him ship-shape for our journey. Reckons he's in love, but I know better. I'll see you back here at two tomorrow.

DECKER *goes*.

TURNER. Thank you.

THOMAS. Men of our class must stick together. Tomorrow then.

TURNER. Yes, tomorrow.

THOMAS *hands back* TURNER*'s sketches*.

THOMAS. These aren't bad, you know. Really, they're not bad at all.

TURNER. Little hobby of mine.

THOMAS. You've captured the moment.

TURNER. Just a hobby. I hope to get better with practice.

Scene Four

1840. London. Outside a hovel in the East End. MEG sits on an upturned bucket smoking a pipe. JESS comes out of the house wearing a 'ballgown' – it is made up of a patchwork of stitched-together rags. Her mother LUCY follows with pins in her mouth. MEG can speak and understand English, but refuses to. She speaks with an African accent to denote her speaking another tongue.

JESS. Where's Papa? Isn't he back yet? I want to show him.

LUCY. Still, Jess. You don't want them pins to prick you.

JESS. I wanna show everyone. (*She spins around.*) Am I beautiful?

MEG (*admiring* JESS). Oooh!

JESS. Do I look like a princess? Am I to be the belle of the ball?

LUCY. Now everybody's seen you get back inside. It's bad luck to be so showy-offy.

MEG (*African*). You should have seen the way we dressed for the ceremony of women. Oh, yes. I had a skirt made of woven straw. It looked like spun gold. And the older women had skirts of peacock feathers, which when they span – and they could all spin even well into old age – was a whir of colour.

JESS. Whas she say, Mum?

LUCY. Never you mind.

JESS. Will I be the belle of the ball, Mama?

LUCY. You won't be anything, you don't keep still.

MEG (*African*). The men too were beautiful. You couldn't see their faces, though, because they wore masks they had fashioned from clay then stained with colours that corresponded to the various river gods.

JESS. You practise the quadrille with me?

LUCY. You know I don't dance. Still now, Jess. And silent. I've to concentrate.

MEG (*African*). I could teach you all a dance to bring out the power of the storm gods. I will teach you a dance to excite the wrath of Mumbi, the goddess of the earth. It will happen, I warn you. They will have their revenge one day for the afflictions visited on their children.

JESS. What language she speaking?

LUCY. Speak English, Meg. I know you can.

JESS. Wish I had a secret language.

LUCY. What for? What secrets you got?

JESS. We've all got secrets, Mama, don't we? Desires.

LUCY. What secret desires you got?

JESS. Won't be a secret if I tell you, would it?

LUCY. I know what you dream about. Same's all young girls dream about. It's not what you wish it to be, believe me.

JESS. I don't dream about those things, not me. Promise you won't laugh.

LUCY. When did you last hear me laugh?

JESS. I dream of the sea, of being a sailor like Papa was.

LUCY. You and your stories.

JESS. You said you wouldn't laugh.

LUCY. A sailor. It isn't how your father tells it, believe me. For a start it's freezing. And I know how much you hate the cold.

JESS. I'd get used to it. I want adventures. I want something to happen to me.

LUCY. You want something to happen to you. It already has, believe me.

JESS. What? What? Why are you always laughing at me? I'm not a child any more, Mama.

LUCY. Then stop behaving like one.

BENJAMIN *the beggar enters. He wears a model of a ship on his head.*

BENJAMIN. Aye-aye! Wait till you see what I've got for you.

MEG. Oh no, it's him. I mustn't let him find me.

MEG runs off.

LUCY. Come back, Meg. It's only Benjamin. You've scared her off, look.

BENJAMIN. Every single time.

LUCY. Thinks you've come to bring her back to her old master. (*To* MEG *who has disappeared inside.*) Slavery is abolished, Meg.

BENJAMIN. Beggars can't be choosers I suppose.

LUCY. What you want, Benjamin? You come to give back what you stole from me?

BENJAMIN. I ain't stole nothing. I'm a beggar not a thief.

LUCY. Then you made enough today to give me back what you owe us? I know how much you lot earn from begging.

BENJAMIN. Begging is noble and skilled work. I come from a long line of mendicants going back to the Romans.

LUCY. That ain't how Thomas tells it.

Another beggar, PETER PIPER, *enters, also wearing a ship on his head and dressed with exactly the same studied dishevelment as* BENJAMIN.

PETER. The scriptures say 'give generously to the poor and do so without a grudging heart'.

BENJAMIN. Peter Piper. What you doing round here?

PETER. I could ask you the same question.

BENJAMIN. As you can see I'm paying a visit to my family. You following me, Peter?

PETER. No.

BENJAMIN. You'd better not be. You know what happened the last time. I knocked you flat.

PETER. I'm not following yer. I took a detour. I got lost…

BENJAMIN. I knocked you flat, and I'd do it again.

PETER. There'll be no fighting. I am a man of peace.

LUCY. You never told us you had a twin brother.

BENJAMIN. He's an upstart. He's copied my style (*To*
PETER.) I've told you a million times that this is my turf.
I've even drawn up the beggars' maps for you, marked out
our relevant areas of business.

PETER. Just because you put marks on a map don't give you
ownership.

BENJAMIN. The area from Blackbird Gardens to Black Boy
Lane belongs to me. You see anywhere on that map marked
Whiteboy Lane?

PETER. No.

BENJAMIN. Then get out of it.

PETER. We've all got a living to make, Benji.

BENJAMIN. He's no black man. He's white as snow. Blackens
his face with coal of a morning then goes out robbing the
food from our baby's mouths. Away with yer, you're not
welcome here. I used to be a boxer – you've no doubt heard
of me... Black-knuckle Ben – and, so help me, I'll knock
you flat I ever see you round here again.

PETER. All right, all right I'm going. But I'd just like to point
out that everyone from these parts is in the same boat.
Poverty strikes us all the same way.

BENJAMIN. Were you ever held in the hold of a ship, packed
in so tight you had another man's arse in your face?

PETER. Well no, but...

BENJAMIN. Did you ever stand in an auction block while men
bid for you like they'd bid for a cow at market?

PETER. Well no, but...

BENJAMIN. You ever worked on a plantation under the hot sun
without water all day, your skin blistered and had an

overseer whip you back on your feet when you fainted? And
this for all, women and children, both.

PETER. No, but I – and others like me – are as good as slaves.
Work our fingers to the bone to keep the rich man happy. We
earn next to nothing.

*The others start to laugh, as he makes his speech they laugh
harder, drowning him out.*

Yes, for next to nothing, like slaves. Servants at the beck and
call of the hoity-toity who can dispose of our efforts at will.
Oh, you can laugh, but you know that I'm telling the truth.

LUCY. Get you gone, Peter. You've given us a good laugh
today, but enough now.

PETER. I don't know what you're all laughing at. I'm telling
the truth and you know it. Think you're special, you lot,
don't yer? Well, you're not.

They're still laughing.

BENJAMIN. You still here, Peter Piper?

PETER. Who's gonna make me leave?

BENJAMIN *puts up his fists and starts to shadow box with*
PETER *who didn't expect this.* PETER *runs away from him.*

Why pick on me? What I done to you? You've got a fury in
you, youse lot. Whatever you're angry about I ain't the one
to blame.

BENJAMIN. Enough excuses. Get you gone, you thieving git.

PETER *goes.*

Thieving bastard. Steal my costume? This is my livelihood.

LUCY. You're as big a liar as he is. You was never enslaved.

BENJAMIN. We are all enslaved, Lucy. It is a question of
degree. Look at Thomas: gone to sign up as a body servant,
has he? Nowadays they pay us a pittance to do with our
bodies what they used to do for free.

BENJAMIN *guffaws.*

LUCY. Get away with you and your dirty mind.

THOMAS *enters*.

THOMAS. What's dirty? You calling me names again, Luce?

JESS. Papa. I missed you. Mama's being horrid.

THOMAS. Steady on. I've only been gone two minutes.

LUCY. Signed up, did you?

THOMAS. I did. There's a catch, though.

LUCY. What's that then?

THOMAS. Man I'm working for is going on a trip.

LUCY. Those toffs are always gadding about. And they expect
the body servant to go with them. You know that.

THOMAS. This isn't just any old trip. He made mention of
a voyage...

JESS. Across the sea?

THOMAS. A long voyage, he says. And I'm to go with him.

LUCY. Tell him no.

THOMAS. I can't do that. I'm signed up. Signed a contract.

LUCY. Then unsign. Scratch your name off that contract.
You're not going.

THOMAS (*tender*). You said yourself I've no choice. It's part
of my job now.

LUCY. When're you going?

THOMAS. Tomorrow. So you'd better make the best of your
old pappy till then.

JESS. You'll be back for the ball of blacks, though?

THOMAS. I'll bring you back a bale of silk so you'll have
a fine gown for the next one.

JESS. I'll stow away in the hold and go with you.

LUCY. You'll do no such thing. Stow away in the hold... what do you know about a filthy hold? Get away inside with yer.

JESS. It was only talk.

THOMAS. There's no need to be so harsh with the girl.

LUCY. I'll have no talk of voyages or holds from either of you. Take that dress off, Jess. I've not finished it. It'll fall apart.

JESS. Do you like my ballgown, Pap?

THOMAS. There's a whole world in that dress. My life and Lucy's laid out like a map. You're a beauty for sure.

JESS. I wish you'd see me at the ball.

THOMAS. I'll be there in spirit.

LUCY. I thought I told you to go inside and take that off.

JESS goes.

BENJAMIN. I have your tickets for the ball of blacks.

Gives THOMAS the tickets.

THOMAS. The cost?

BENJAMIN. Don't insult me, brother. You can stand me an ale.

THOMAS. I'll stand you two ales.

BENJAMIN salutes and goes.

LUCY. I've never known you to tell a lie, Tommy.

THOMAS. And I never will.

LUCY. You've signed articles, haven't you? I seen that hunger in you. Heard it rumbling through your body.

THOMAS. I didn't lie to you.

LUCY. Soon as you left I knew. I'm the one's a liar. You'd no more be a servant than I would.

THOMAS. This will be the last time. I can promise you that at least.

LUCY. Where to this time?

THOMAS. Africa. They're trading cloth, coffee and sweetmeats.

LUCY *laughs*.

LUCY. And so it continues. Get the African to produce sugar and cotton; seed in them a desire for the goods you produce from them – fine cloths, sugar… then sell them back what they sweated to create. You are not going to find it. Whatever it is that you are seeking. That missing part of yourself that you long for is gone. There's no compass in your mind to lead you back to the home you've lost. And you tell me to forget? I'm the one should seek articles. You have a brother here. Nursed your father when he died. What have I got? I had other children, Thomas.

THOMAS. You torture yourself.

LUCY. The youngest was sold to a lady bought him as a pet for her own son. Put a silver collar on him before she took him away. I seen the way they treat their dogs: feed them roast beef and give 'em duck-feather cushions to sleep on. And I told myself my baby'd have a better life because he'd be treated like a dog.

THOMAS. He'll be grown now. He's free.

LUCY. Free, is he? Like you? Like me?

THOMAS. We must try to forget.

LUCY. How do I do that? How do I make myself forget? The past is branded all over my body. You cannot bear the sight of me. That is why you run away.

THOMAS. That's not true.

LUCY. You cannot bear to look at or touch me.

THOMAS. I am looking at you.

He moves towards LUCY *and takes hold of her from behind. She squirms. He pulls at her dress and kisses her shoulder where she has been branded.*

I am touching you. I long for this. To hold you, to smell you. It is you who hide yourself from me.

He pulls at her dress and kisses her shoulder.

This brand has no meaning any more. What it once stood for no longer exists.

LUCY. I recall the fire of this branding, the smell of my own roasting flesh. I remember it all. It is an ugly thing.

THOMAS. It is a sign of what you have survived, that through it all you remained human and tender.

LUCY (*emotional*). She put a collar on my boy and took him away to her own child. She had no milk to feed him. How could he grow without milk, Thomas?

LUCY *pulls herself together.*

THOMAS. You have my love.

LUCY. Yes.

THOMAS. Despite all we've been through there is still love between us. Jess is the proof.

LUCY. So many of the women on that plantation were barren. As though the hardship had killed their bodies. Every time the man who called himself their master beat them to make them breed he stunted their bodies even more.

THOMAS. Every time we remember that the love is a real thing between us, then your boy lives.

LUCY. I remember the softness of him, the tickle of his little mouth latched onto my breast, his curled fingers reaching for me.

THOMAS. I love you, Lucy. And our Jess.

LUCY. You put ideas in that girl's head.

THOMAS. She is a person. People have dreams.

LUCY. Dreams can kill a soul.

THOMAS *kisses the mark where* LUCY *has been branded.*

THOMAS. You are more than this, Lucy.

Pause. A moment between THOMAS *and* LUCY.

LUCY. I'll let you go, Thomas. I'll not hold you back.

THOMAS. And when I return there'll be an end to it. No more wandering. We'll have a new beginning.

Scene Five

2006. Rehearsal room. Same day as Scene One.

JEANIE (*reading*). Interior, Turner's Studio. Night. Turner comes into the room in his nightdress.

ROY. That's gonna be interesting.

The others laugh.

JEANIE. The sound of something scuttling across the room.

ROY (*as* TURNER). Who's there? I know you're there, I heard you.

JEANIE (*reading*). Turner lights a candle and uses it to illuminate a corner of the room. Olu appears, naked, wet.

LOU. Naked? Is that new?

TREVOR. It was in the script I sent you.

LOU. Oh.

TREVOR. Shall we go from Turner 'I thought you had gone away.'

ROY. Ready, Lou?

LOU. Yes-yes.

ROY. I thought you had gone away. Now that I have told your story.

JEANIE. Olu stands to face him.

LOU. It is a beautiful painting.

ROY. I have merely painted what you described to me.

LOU. It will speak down the ages.

ROY. Tell me, spirit, why did you choose me?

LOU. Ghosts are brought forth from the imagination, are they not?

ROY. So, Turner is mad?

LOU. The unburied are restless.

ROY. The unburied...

LOU. You told my story – the story of the *Zong* massacre. And now I can be laid to rest.

JEANIE (*reading*). Olu disappears. Turner is surprised, disappointed. He turns to the covered canvas, removes the sheet to reveal the painting *The Slave Ship*. Ends.

Those around the table applaud.

ROY. Well done, Trevor. It's a beautiful piece.

LOU. Sorry-sorry, but the script's changed since I first read it.

TREVOR. There have been a few changes, yes.

LOU. Olu feels different in this draft.

TREVOR. Let's have a break. Then we can chat.

The crew, etc. go off to have coffee/biscuits. LOU *and* TREVOR *are left alone.* REUBEN *also hangs back.*

LOU. What happened to all that wonderful material about Olu's life before she was captured?

TREVOR. They asked for cuts.

LOU. Who asked? It's your film, isn't it?

TREVOR. It undermined the intensity of the massacre and I wanted that to –

LOU. The audience has to identify with her as a person. They have to be invested. Otherwise, they won't feel the impact of her death. It's supposed to be her story.

TREVOR. The film is – and always has been – about the painting. That was my starting point. I asked myself how he came to paint such a thing. The audience will feel cheated if we don't give them an answer. Roy told me...

LOU. Roy? Oh, I see…

TREVOR. Roy didn't think Turner was rounded enough. He's more complex in this version.

LOU. Well, I'm asking for changes too.

TREVOR. It's not a free-for-all, Lou.

LOU. My ideas are as valid as Roy's.

REUBEN. You got rid of all those amazing scenes about the Sons of Africa.

TREVOR. Don't you start. The conditions for the grant from the Abolition Legacy Foundation require that the film commemorates the bicentenary of abolition.

REUBEN. And abolition was all about the heroism of white people?

TREVOR. Of course not.

REUBEN. Did you read any of those books I gave you?

LOU. My name carries as much clout as Roy's. Change the script, give her back her story or I'm walking.

TREVOR. Which would you prefer? That the film got made, that people get to hear a story that most of them have never heard before, or that the script disappears?

LOU. You won't disappear, Trevor. You're a survivor that's for sure.

TREVOR. Don't mess this up for me. We might never get an opportunity like this again. It's all right for you: You made it in the States, that means you can come back and pick and choose your projects. It's not like that for the rest of us.

LOU. It's bad enough that you've got me playing a ghost. A fucking ghost, Trev.

LOU *laughs*.

TREVOR *laughs nervously*.

TREVOR. We shouldn't let them see us arguing.

LOU. Why not? We're people. People argue.

TREVOR. They'll say we're being unprofessional.

LOU. A ghost, for fuck's sake. We're always playing ghosts in one way or another. We're not seen as real functioning people. When is this shit going to stop? Exactly what is it that is so hard for the British public to hear? That the British did in fact enslave and trade black people? That the *Zong* massacre was not a one-off event? You and I – the descendants of slaves – we've got a duty to tell that story.

ROY enters. Pause.

ROY. Can I get you a cup of tea?

LOU. I'm all right, Roy.

ROY. Coming to lunch? I've booked us a table.

LOU. I'll be there in a minute.

ROY. Deanne was over the moon when I told her you're doing this. She was just saying the other day that we should have you over for supper again.

LOU. Yes, I'd like that.

Pause. Aware of the awkwardness, ROY *leaves. Pause.*

TREVOR. Promise me you won't sabotage the project.

LOU. Give me a reason not to.

TREVOR. I'll take another look at the script. I don't want to lose you, Lou.

TREVOR leaves.

LOU. Thank you for backing me up.

REUBEN. We shouldn't be too hard on him. He's trying to please everyone.

LOU. You know, Reuben, there are days when I really do feel like a ghost. When I'm the only person who looks like me sat around a table at a read-through. I hear people say, 'She's more successful than most. She's made a bit of money.

What exactly is her problem? Haven't we given her enough?'
The answer to that is no. No it isn't nearly enough.

Pause.

REUBEN. Would you like to… do you want me to go over the
research material with you? We could find a nice bar, just
chill, you know.

LOU. All right. Yes. Yes I'd like that.

Pause. They hold each other's gaze, smile.

Scene Six

1840. The docks. THOMAS *is with* JESS *and* LUCY. *He is
waiting to board the ship –* The Glory *– as a sailor.*

JESS. Look at her sails, and her masts. She's like a lady in
a fine ballgown. Her name suits her: *The Glory.* You'll bring
me back beautiful silks to make a gown with?

THOMAS. I shall bring you back gold and diamonds, and silk
for a gown.

LUCY. You spoil the girl.

THOMAS. Look after your mother when I've gone. I know
she's a pain in the arse sometimes but under all that bluster
she's a good heart.

LUCY. A strong heart. I need one to put up with you.

JESS (*giggles*). Do I have to stay? I want to come with you.

THOMAS. You'll be a sailor, will you? A life at sea is not for
a girl.

LUCY. Not unless they've shackled you in the hold, all of you
together – men, women, children – cheek by jowl; up to your
neck in somebody else's shit and vomit, not to mention the
stink of the festering sores carved out on your back by the cat.

THOMAS. Will you stop, woman? What does this child know about whips and chains? She was born free and will remain so.

Sound of a ship's horn.

LUCY. Don't go, Thomas. Not onto that ship.

THOMAS. You said I should go.

LUCY. I didn't know you were going on *The Glory*. I can't bear to look at it. It is cursed. I don't want you getting on it.

JESS. What's she talking about, Papa?

LUCY. We promised each other we'd never set foot on a slavers' ship ever again.

JESS. A slaver?

THOMAS. Used to be, and is no more.

LUCY. They've given it a new name, scrubbed it clean, removed the shackles from its hold, but they can't get rid of the stench. Smell it miles off.

JESS. Papa. Please don't get on it. Please. Please don't get on it. I beg you, Papa. (JESS *is crying*.)

THOMAS. See what you've done. How can I leave you both like this?

LUCY. Then don't go.

THOMAS. It calls to me. I can't stay away. The sea is in my blood. I am a sailor after all.

LUCY. Didn't we make a promise to ourselves that we would never again make such a journey?

JESS. The ship is cursed, Papa. Don't go. Don't leave us.

THOMAS. Whenever you feel that you are missing me come here, to the water. Whisper a message and the river will carry it to the sea, who will carry it to the ocean, who will carry it to me.

JESS. All the way to Africa? Can you swim, Pappy?

THOMAS. Of course I can swim.

JESS. How come you can swim and I can't?

LUCY. You'd swim if you had to. It comes natural to a body in danger.

JESS. I have a fear of drowning. I've drowned in my dreams several times. I'm devilish cold, Pappy.

THOMAS. Hark at you, my little lady. Devilish cold is it? Which pocket?

JESS chooses a pocket.

The sound of the ship's horn again.

THOMAS searches in another pocket and fetches out a small sugar stick and gives it to her.

LUCY. Sugar? You're giving her sugar?

THOMAS. It is all right to eat sugar now.

LUCY. Not for me. It is bitter aloes in my mouth. Always will be.

JESS happily takes the sugar and sucks on it.

THOMAS. I shall stand on the deck to watch you. I don't want to see you crying, mind.

He kisses both of them then leaves. JESS and LUCY are distraught. LUCY pulls herself together. She wipes away JESS's tears.

LUCY. Wave and smile. It'll make him sad if he sees you crying when the ship leaves harbour.

JESS. You said the ship is cursed.

LUCY. How can a ship be cursed? I only said it to make him stay. Smile and wave, Jess, smile and wave.

JESS. How can I smile when my heart is breaking?

LUCY. There he is. Wave, Jess, wave. We'll count the days together till he returns. We'll send him messages in bottles. You've a sugar stick to comfort you.

The ship's horn blows. JESS takes her mother's hand. They wave as the ship departs.

Scene Seven

The film set: Late 1781 on board the Zong. *OLU (LOU), shackled and on her knees with two sailors –* PEARSON *and* JOHNSON *– either side of her.*

JOHNSON. She danced?

PEARSON. I made sure of that.

JOHNSON. But won't eat? You talk to her?

PEARSON. Tried several tongues. She don't answer.

JOHNSON. She mute?

PEARSON. I've seen her in the hold, whispering to the other women.

JOHNSON (*to* OLU). You'll need your strength if you're planning an insurrection.

PEARSON. She don't understand you.

JOHNSON. Captain thinks they're feeble-minded, but I know better. Last ship I was on they mutinied and tried to steer a way back to Africa. They'd watched the stars and knew the route better than the sextant – (*To* OLU.) Learned English too in the weeks at sea.

PEARSON. The only insurrection this one's plotting is to starve her way to the ancestors. Look at her, skin and bones.

JOHNSON. I spend so much time in that mucky hold that I might as well be a slave myself. I keep you exercised, oiled, fed and ready for auction. You will not die on my watch. You die I forfeit my wages. Pass the dabadab.

PEARSON *passes* JOHNSON *a bucket of mush made of grain and various seeds.* JOHNSON *spoons mush and tries to feed it to* OLU *who refuses it. She bites* JOHNSON*'s hand. He screams.*

You'll eat and Madam Oris will make sure that you do.

JOHNSON *takes a speculum oris from the belt that he is wearing. He gives* PEARSON *the nod.* OLU *puts up a furious fight, but* PEARSON *holds her head while* JOHNSON *forces the speculum into her mouth and down into her throat. He tightens the screw on the speculum, ensuring that her throat remains open while he spoons the dabadab into her mouth. He stands back and watches as she gurgles and struggles, refuses the mush by vomiting it out.*

I'll make you eat. (*To* PEARSON.) The cat.

PEARSON. Why don't we try one more time…

JOHNSON. It's our job to season her. By the end of this voyage she'll be a slave.

PEARSON *fetches the cat and gives it to* JOHNSON *who starts to whip* OLU *with it.* OLU *flinches with the pain of every lash. The beating becomes more severe as* JOHNSON *gets caught up in it. In a fit of fury* OLU *grabs the whip from him and turns it on him, beating him. Shocked, he cries out.*

Oi! Fucking hell, Lou. What's going on? That ain't in the script.

TREVOR *enters.*

LOU *continues to beat* JOHNSON. PEARSON *holds her back. It is as though she is possessed. She starts to calm down.*

PEARSON. You all right?

JOHNSON. Yes, I'm all right.

TREVOR. What the hell was that, Lou?

LOU. I'm sorry. Sorry-sorry. For a moment there, I thought…

JOHNSON. You got a bit carried away there

LOU. Sorry-sorry. It was a joke, a prank. I was just joking, having you on.

There is a pause at first and then everyone starts to laugh.

JOHNSON. You got me. Thought you was trying to make some kind of point.

LOU. I was joking. Sorry.

JOHNSON. No, it was funny. It was funny. We're laughing…

TREVOR. Let's take a break. We'll come back to it.

REUBEN *comes on*.

REUBEN. Are you all right, Lou?

LOU. I'm fine.

JOHNSON. I hate doing that with the cat.

LOU. It's all right. I don't feel anything.

JOHNSON. I know but… It makes me feel like a… like a…
It makes me feel like a… See you after lunch.

PEARSON *and* JOHNSON *go off*.

TREVOR. Lou?

LOU. Honestly, I'm all right. I just need a minute.

TREVOR *goes*.

I took this job because I thought Trevor got away from the
usual torture porn: A black body gets a whipping. Check.
A black body is sold at auction. Check. White people getting
off on the sentimental horror while every single lash of that
whip sends home a subliminal message that to be white
means to have never been a slave.

REUBEN. Our history, hidden in plain sight, the white
abolitionists' story squashing the story of the Africans who
spoke up, who alerted the public to the massacre in the first
place. We did not make you suffer. We do not make you
suffer. It is over now. Over and done with. I read between the
lines of the books you gave me. I'm trying to hear those
people whose stories have been erased.

REUBEN *notices what looks like blood on* LOU*'s shirt*.

Your back. There's blood on your shirt. Those fuckers really
hurt you.

LOU. Nothing it's nothing. The doctor says that it's an allergic
reaction.

REUBEN. That's some allergy.

LOU. He says it's because I'm not sleeping… I've got a lot on my mind… My granddad's ill. I've neglected him.

REUBEN. You've been working. He'll understand. I'll bet he's really proud of you.

LOU. They don't think he's going to last much longer.

REUBEN. I'm sorry.

LOU. I have to go and see him.

REUBEN. Of course. I'll come with you if you like.

LOU. That's kind, but I have to go on my own.

REUBEN. You weren't in bed when I woke up last night. I found you at the window staring at the river.

LOU. I can't remember.

REUBEN. You sleep walk. (*Slight pause.*) It looks painful, Lou. You should put some cream or something on it.

LOU. It's all right. I'm all right, Reuben.

REUBEN. I'm sorry we're putting you through this.

REUBEN *lifts her shirt and blows on her back.*

LOU. They can see you.

REUBEN. I don't care. I want them to see me.

LOU. Honestly, I'm okay.

REUBEN. I know you are.

LOU. You won't tell Trevor or Roy? Promise? They won't understand. They think this is just history, but it isn't.

REUBEN. Then what is it? If it isn't history what is it?

Scene Eight

2007. Street. A group of people walk across the stage memorialising a mock Coffle Walk.

ESSIE. Come on, Billie. Keep up.

BILLIE. Do I look like a slave to you? Does my mum look like a slave? My sister, my uncles, my auntie. They look like slaves to you?

ESSIE. That's not the point, Billie. And you know it.

BILLIE. What is the point then? Yeah. No point. It's fuckeries, miss.

ESSIE. You feel what they – the enslaved – you get a feeling for what they went through.

BILLIE. Why I wanna do that? They wouldn't want me to do that. That woman told us. She told us how people used to jump in the sea and fly to their ancestors rather than be captured. So you tell me why someone who flew to their ancestors would want me to go on a Coffle Walk?

ESSIE. It's to honour them. A memorial... We pay tribute to the dead because they weren't ever afforded the dignity of burial rites...

BILLIE. Fuckeries, miss. I'm not moving from here. You can exclude me or whatever.

ESSIE. Stop swearing, Billie.

　　BILLIE *scribbles over his picture with his pencil. Then he angrily bangs his clipboard on the ground, tears the pad from the clipboard and scatters the pages.* ESSIE *picks up the pages.*

　　I'm not scared of you, Billie. Not everybody who looks at you sees what you think they see.

BILLIE. How d'you know what I think they see?

ESSIE. Oh, I know. Don't destroy the gifts you've been given, Billie.

　　BILLIE *helps* ESSIE *to pick up the loose pages.*

BILLIE. You're nice, miss.

ESSIE. Oh, Billie.

BILLIE. You are. You're always kind to us.

ESSIE. That's because I think you're special.

BILLIE. Special? Me?

ESSIE. Haven't you noticed how the others look up to you?

BILLIE. I'm not special, miss.

ESSIE. No?

BILLIE. Well, maybe a bit.

ESSIE. Come on, let's join the others.

BILLIE. Do we have to?

ESSIE. Don't you want to know where you come from?

BILLIE. I don't come from that, miss. I wouldn't let no one imprison me.

ESSIE. I'll do a deal with you. Stick this out and I'll let you have the art room all to yourself for an hour after school on Tuesdays.

BILLIE *doesn't respond.*

All you have to do is stick it out for the rest of the day.

BILLIE. All I have to do is stay here till the end of the day?

ESSIE. All the colour you want. Canvases. Charcoal, pastels and nobody looking over your shoulder. If you rebel everybody else will. They look up to you. You might not need this history, but they do. They need to experience that trip up the river, to take part in a Coffle Walk.

ESSIE *picks up another page torn from* BILLIE*'s sketchbook.* BILLIE *watches as she gently smoothes it out.*

BILLIE. Tuesdays and Thursdays.

ESSIE *hands* BILLIE *the broken clipboard. He takes it.*

Scene Nine

1840. On board The Glory. TURNER *alone on the deck,*
watching the sea, sketching. Because he is alone he has
dropped his pretence of having one arm. From below we can
hear the SAILORS *carousing – drumming, drinking and*
singing. MARY *is also on deck. She has a mermaid's tail. As*
she speaks THOMAS *comes onto the deck, wearing a mask,*
and watches. There is also a large tub of water on deck.

MARY. The day you was born was unbearably hot and as
I pushed you out the room was illuminated with light. You
certainly did not look extraordinary. You was not pretty like
my girl had been. You had the look of a squealing piglet.
Once I'd suckled and lain you in your basket I went to the
window and looked out. The world was different. There was
two suns in the sky. Even though the scientists said it was a
mirage, a distortion of light caused by ice crystals formed of
cold air, I knew it was all down to me.

THOMAS. What kind of magic is this?

TURNER (*surprised, stops sketching*). You see her too, do you?

THOMAS. I see her all right. An arm where there used to be
a stump.

TURNER. Oh – (*Looks at his arm.*) Oh shit. Please, don't tell
anyone.

THOMAS. What are you, mister?

TURNER. I… I make pictures. I've always had the knack and
make a few pennies by sketching for people. All my life
I dreamed of being a sailor. You don't begrudge an old man
his last chance for the sea, do you?

THOMAS. You are a man of secrets.

TURNER. Promise you won't tell. It's carnage down there.

THOMAS. It is an ancient rite, that's all. There's no harm in it.

TURNER. They'll destroy me.

THOMAS. Draw me.

TURNER. I'm better at the elements than people.

THOMAS goes to put his mask on. TURNER *quickly starts to sketch* THOMAS.

I'm grateful for the extra rations – (*Raises his pint mug.*) You drunk yet?

THOMAS. Getting there. You?

TURNER *sways on his feet.*

TURNER. I'm there.

THOMAS. Listen-listen. The mermaids are singing.

Sound of whale music.

TURNER (*listens*). Oh yes. Never heard that before.

TURNER *starts to sketch* THOMAS *in silence.*

MARY. My father – your grandfather – was a butcher so I was used to seeing animal cadavers, but one day I went down to where they stored the meat and I saw men hanging from the hooks, their eyes open, staring at me and all the blood drained from them. When I went back upstairs and told them what I'd seen they said that I had imagined it and that there was nothing there.

TURNER *is having trouble with the sketch. He scribbles over the sketch and throws the page away.*

TURNER. Tell me a secret. Tell me about your woman.

S*light pause as* THOMAS *recalls a memory.* TURNER *starts to sketch.*

THOMAS. Met my Lucy on a slave ship. She was an enslaved woman imprisoned in the hold. I'd bring her my rations, keep the other sailors away from her. When we got to Jamaica I knew that I could not leave without her, so I gave the captain a promissory note, pledged him my labour for so many voyages, and bought her. She come back to London with me and I give her a choice: you can stay here with me, or you can leave. She stayed. And when she learned to speak English she told me she had stayed just so that she could tell me that I did not, could not own her.

TURNER. She's fiery then.

THOMAS. I'll say.

TURNER. The best sort.

The men laugh, both drunk now. TURNER *hands* THOMAS *the sketch.* THOMAS *looks at it then hands it back.*

THOMAS. That don't look like me.

TURNER. Your face has a peculiar mobility. I couldn't capture it.

THOMAS. Now you. Tell me a secret.

TURNER *starts to clean his brushes.*

MARY. He ain't got the nerve. He knows the meaning of the vision I had in that cellar, but he won't tell. He'll take his secrets to the grave, that one.

TURNER. Shut up and leave me alone. Who asked you?

THOMAS. No need for that.

TURNER. Sorry-sorry. Too much of this – (*Refers to drink.*) A secret you say… All right: When I was a kid you'd see them… you'd see the sugar barons going about in their golden carriages, wealthier than the king himself. So, when I started to make money I invested in a sugar works. Didn't make a penny. It was very badly managed.

THOMAS. A sugar works? What used the free labour of Africans?

TURNER. Now, don't… don't go all.

THOMAS. The free labour of Africans?

TURNER. You can talk. Didn't you purchase your Lucy?…

THOMAS. I bought her freedom. I didn't… Did you think that I…

TURNER. I was young… I didn't think it through. All my old friends were abolitionists. Stanhope, Clarkson. Great men. My name is Joseph Mallord William Turner. I am an artist, a member of the Royal Academy.

THOMAS *laughs.*

THOMAS. You mad old git. The sea wine's gone to your head. You ain't got a pot to piss in much less the money to invest in a sugar works. (*Refers to picture.*) This don't even look like me.

TURNER. Yes-yes. Too much wine.

THOMAS. Invested in a sugar works… You're just an old pollywog.

TURNER. That's right. Just an old…

THOMAS *puts on his mask.*

TURNER. What? No. Please don't… please.

THOMAS. POLLYWOG!

The other SAILORS *rush on deck, all wearing strange costumes and masks, dressed as Neptune's helpers. They have all had too much grog.* DECKER *enters dressed as King Neptune. He carries a broom made into a trident and wears a crown fashioned from a metal dish.*

CAESAR. Bow before King Neptune. A pollywog must not look at the King of the Sea –

TURNER *bows his head.*

NEPTUNE *ceremoniously takes his place on deck.*

DECKER. Bring me the pollywog!

The SAILORS *put a blind and gag on* TURNER *then spin him around. They lift him and pass him along the deck until he is standing before* DECKER.

You are charged with crossing the line into my waters without qualification. What do you plead?

TURNER *tries to speak through the gag. The* SAILORS *turn him around. He falls to his feet disorientated.*

He pleads guilty. He will be made to drink divine waters from the sea. Bring him the sea wine.

SAILORS *hand along a cup of grog, each subjecting it to a different defilement – one man spits in it, another stirs in*

*a bogey, yet another farts into the cup, etc. The cup arrives
at* TURNER *who is made to drink the sea wine. He almost
retches, but drinks it down. They pat him on the back, while
singing.*

The SAILORS *carry on a plank and hold it on the edge
of the tub. The rest of the* SAILORS *lift* TURNER *onto
the plank.*

DECKER. Now, able seaman pollywog, now that you are
shrived by Neptune. You will cross the line over the equator.

TURNER. I can't see nothing.

DECKER. As you cross the line Neptune will give you new
eyes, sir. Walk.

A SAILOR *prods* TURNER *and he starts to walk across the
plank, feeling with his feet. He slips and the* SAILORS *cheer,
lift him up and dunk his head into the tub of water. He yells,
which seems to amuse them even more and they dunk him
a few more times before setting him on his feet before Neptune.*

Now you may look upon Neptune, your God.

The blindfold and gag are removed.

Do you swear allegiance to Neptune's laws?

TURNER. Eh?

DECKER. It's a simple question. Do you swear allegiance to
Neptune's laws?

TURNER. I swear, yes I swear.

DECKER. Now I proclaim you a shellback, a son of Neptune.

The SAILORS *cheer and carry* TURNER *on their backs.
More drumming and singing.* TURNER *is set back on his
feet. Another shout issues from below deck.*

SAILOR. POLLYWOG!

DECKER and the SAILORS *rush below.* TURNER *and*
THOMAS *remain on stage.* THOMAS *takes his mask off.
A crack of thunder – the men stand staring at each other.*

ACT TWO

Scene Ten

1840. Cape Coast. Night. THOMAS *and other* SAILORS *are unloading the last of the goods to be traded, overseen by* DECKER. *A banging issues from inside the ship.*

THOMAS. What's all the noise?

DECKER. She's having repairs done. It's impossible for an old girl like her to make a long voyage like this one without damage. I reckon this is her last. Her owners should cut their losses. They've had enough out of her. That's the last of it.

THOMAS (*looking into the hold*). What's this, Decker? They're fitting her with chains.

DECKER. Don't worry yourself with that.

A COFFLE OF ENCHAINED AFRICANS *has arrived on stage.* BILLIE *is enchained with them as is* CAESAR *the shantyman. The* SAILORS *have seen them and a general dismay passes over the crew.*

If I was you I'd mind me own beeswax. (*To* SAILORS.) Get them on board.

The SAILORS *load them onto the ship, ushering them into the hold.*

THOMAS. I didn't sign to a ship that trades in flesh. This is wrong.

DECKER. Not where we're going, it isn't. Captain says we're changing course. We're bound for Brazil.

THOMAS. This wasn't in the articles.

DECKER. What business is it of yours what we trade in?

THOMAS. I signed up for a merchant voyage.

DECKER. And what do you think this is?

THOMAS. I'll not serve on this ship. Where's the captain? He'll want to know about your deception

DECKER. Who do you think paid for all this? Me? I'm not ashamed to say that I've drunk all my profit.

THOMAS. Slavery is abolished.

DECKER. Tell that to the captain. His family owned plantations in Jamaica. This is the only business he knows. Me, I just follow orders. What are you all waiting for? Load the ship.

BILLIE *starts to struggle against his chains.*

THOMAS. Let him go. Let them all go.

DECKER. We lose any of these the captain will take the losses out of our wages. That what you want?

THOMAS *pulls* DECKER*'s pistol from his belt and points it at him.*

THOMAS. Give me the keys.

DECKER. They've been marching for days. They're exhausted, poor mites. It'll be a relief for them to settle down below.

THOMAS. Didn't you hear me? Give me the keys.

DECKER *throws the keys down.* THOMAS *unchains* BILLIE *and the others. He holds* BILLIE *by the arm.*

(*To* BILLIE.) You're all right now. I have you.

TURNER *enters unseen by* THOMAS. DECKER *puts on an act for* TURNER.

DECKER. Rob me blind, would you? I should have known not to trust one of your sort.

THOMAS. What's one of my sort, eh, Decker?

DECKER. This instinct for thievery and violence is born in the lot of you. Go on then. I've had enough anyway. Take the ship's cargo and kill me.

TURNER pushes THOMAS and DECKER takes the gun.
They both manhandle THOMAS to the ground while
BILLIE runs away and scuttles up the mast.

Executed like a true shellback. You've scuppered an
insurrection.

THOMAS. You have this all wrong.

They both keep THOMAS pinned to the ground. DECKER
chains his hands behind his back.

BILLIE. They say that Neptune holds dominion over the sea, but
I know that there are other sea gods. The sea talks to me, says
I am not a slave. The sighing waves tell me what I must do.

THOMAS. Don't jump, Billie.

TURNER. Come down, boy.

DECKER. Let him jump. (*Referring to* THOMAS.) This one's
the prize. Skittish as a horse. He'll be seasoned by the time
we get to Brazil.

THOMAS. This ship is not what we thought. They trade in
flesh.

TURNER. I don't want no trouble. I just want to get home.

THOMAS. Flesh, Turner.

TURNER. Do my work.

THOMAS. You are in this, Turner.

TURNER. I am an old man. I make sketches for a few pennies.
That is all.

THOMAS. You are in this. You have a choice to make.

THOMAS is chained and manacled. He screams. They put
a clamp around his mouth.

TURNER. Leave me out of it. It's got nothing to do with me.

Scene Eleven

*2006. The bedroom of a council flat in London. On the bed,
a dying elderly man,* CLARKE. LOU *and her sister* VONNIE
stand watching him. VONNIE *looks like someone who has
just emerged from spending a very long time in the dark into
the light.*

VONNIE. Sorry-sorry. They'll be here in a minute. Auntie
Muriel just texted to say they've been held up on the A22.

LOU. I got a scare. I thought he'd already... You all right?

VONNIE. Yeah. I ain't seen you since...

LOU. Mmmmh.

VONNIE. Sorry about the place.

LOU. That's all right. You've had a lot... There's been a lot.

VONNIE. Yeah.

LOU. You working?

VONNIE. Yeah, yeah... I'm off benefits.

LOU. That's good. That's really good. He'd be proud of you.
You know what he always said about paying your own way,
said they never come over to become charity cases.

VONNIE. You? Still doing the...

LOU. Yeah.

VONNIE. Still doing the...

LOU. I am yes.

VONNIE. Still doing the space stuff, yeah? Cool. Cool. Love it.
I love that show. We all do.

LOU. I'm glad.

VONNIE. You kick arse, man. You tell 'em what's what.

LOU. Try to, yes. Well, the scriptwriters... I advise them,
though. I have a say.

VONNIE. The aliens don't know what's hit 'em when the
captain is on the scene. 'If you don't stand off I will have to
nucleise you.' Nucleise. Love it.

LOU. It's good to see you, Vonnie. I want to say I'm sorry…
For what I said… when we… I was.

VONNIE. I know.

LOU. I was out of order.

VONNIE. You wasn't… What you said was true… I am…
Look at you…

LOU. I apologise…

VONNIE. What for? I am a loser

LOU. Don't… you're… an amazing woman, a beautiful…
you…

VONNIE. Look at you… you've made it…

LOU. Only because… only because you… I'm really grateful
that you've stayed with Mum… everything you've done for
her and Granddad… if you hadn't done that then I couldn't…
I wouldn't have…

VONNIE. No. You worked hard for that. You grafted. Don't
you trash yourself. There's enough people wanting to do that
without you doing it to yourself.

LOU. How long's he been like this?

VONNIE. Last few days. Mum reckons he'll be gone by
morning. She'll be back soon. She's just gone to light
another candle. You know what she's like.

LOU *sobs*.

Don't cry. Not yet. It's his show. If you can't be in the
spotlight on your deathbed when can you be? I'll tell him
you're here. (*Talking to* CLARKE *on the bed*.) Granddad…
It's Captain Sola Andrews.

LOU. For God's sake, Vonnie.

VONNIE. What? He won't remember you.

LOU. But he'll remember Captain Sola Andrews?

VONNIE. He loves that programme. It's the only thing he
watches. Loves it.

VONNIE. Say something.

LOU. What? What shall I say?

VONNIE. Go on. He'll be thrilled that the last words he ever heard were those of Captain Sola Andrews.

LOU. Granddad.

VONNIE. Go on.

LOU. It's Captain Sola Andrews. I don't know what to say.

VONNIE. Tell him about your day... the captain's day.

LOU. Well, we transported these androids to the island of Phobos, but we didn't realise that they had this malware, which made them go against the robotic code of servility. This gave them an instinct for rebellion. This is stupid...

VONNIE. I remember that episode... I've seen it. The ship's transporting captured droids to Phobos and one of the droids escapes and overcomes the captain and frees the other droids. It may be science fiction, but that episode was moving.

CLARKE. Steer a course for Phobos!

VONNIE. Told yer.

LOU. Fucking hell.

VONNIE. Lou. Have some respect for the dying.

LOU. Did you see that, though?

VONNIE. Say something else.

LOU. Energise, Lieutenant. Plot co-ordinates for Phobos.

CLARKE *does not respond.*

VONNIE. Grampy? Granddad?

CLARKE *takes a deep breath. What sounds like the death rattle. Then nothing. Neither of them is sure what to do.*

LOU. Has he gone?

VONNIE. I don't know. Feel for a pulse.

LOU. You feel for a pulse.

VONNIE *feels for a pulse.*

VONNIE. He's still here.

A ring at the doorbell.

That'll be Auntie Muriel.

VONNIE *goes.* LOU *sits. She looks over at her grandfather. She starts to weep. As she does so,* CLARKE *sits up and gets out of the bed.*

CLARKE. You crying, Lou? Now, why you crying?

LOU. Granddad.

CLARKE. The last time you was here…

LOU. It's been a while, Granddad.

CLARKE. We were talking about that ship.

LOU. You've got a better memory than I have.

CLARKE. I will never forget it. What an adventure. I was on that ship for two weeks. There was a party every night. That's how I met your grandmother. In those days I was sharp you see. No wonder she fell in love with me. The best days of my life. It was when we came off the ship that the problems started.

LOU. What problems?

CLARKE. At first it was the snow. One morning I woke up and the street was covered in thick thick snow. Well, I dived right in. Your grandmother thought I was mad, wouldn't join me. But this is how you acclimatise yourself, I said. Just dive in. After that I didn't feel the cold any more, couldn't feel anything. I had become an Englishman. And we worked, Lou. I had three jobs. I worked like a slave.

LOU. I know. You told me, Grampy.

CLARKE. A slave like my grandfather's grandfather. The man who bought him listed him in an inventory of his goods and chattel along with his cows. When they freed those who had been enslaved my grandfather's grandfather continued to work on the plantation. He never spoke of those times before freedom because once he was stripped of personhood it could not be given back to him. He never spoke of where he came from, how he ended up where he did. On his deathbed stories leaked out of him and my grandfather scooped them up as though they were pieces of gold. You know how many laws there are these days to ensure that black people are treated as equals? A real person would not need so many laws. White people think that we are 'like' them, like means not the same: the law says that we are not the same. They used to have the slave codes and now they have equality guidelines.

VONNIE (*calling off*). Lou! Aunt Muriel's here.

CLARKE. You married, Lou? You have someone looking after you?

LOU. I can look after myself. I'm happy, Granddad. Don't you worry about me. You rest yourself.

CLARKE. As long as you're all right...

CLARKE *goes to 'sleep'*. VONNIE *enters*.

VONNIE. Auntie Muriel's outside. She won't come in. Says it's too morbid. Don't know why she bothered coming all this way. What's the matter?

LOU. I was just having a moment.

VONNIE. You two was always thick as thieves. It's the end of an era, Lou.

LOU. It feels like the end of history.

Scene Twelve

2007. Lou's bedroom. LOU *and* MEG.

LOU *is getting ready for the awards ceremony. She is wearing the gown from the prologue. As she gets ready she plays some music (something very contemporary – a garage version of a sea shanty?).* MEG *reacts to the music, nodding, tapping her feet, etc., as she reads from a newspaper.*

MEG (*African accent*). This is good. It reminds me of... of, um... you know... It brings back wonderful memories. Sorry-sorry I should speak English.

LOU (*surprised by herself*). It's all right. I can understand.

MEG (*reads from newspaper*). 'It is hard to believe what would now be a crime against humanity was legal at the time.'

LOU. Who said that? Let me guess: Tony Blair.

MEG. The very same – (*Starts to read again.*) 'It is hard to believe... blah blah... what would now be a crime against humanity was legal at the time.' (*Stops reading.*) But it was a crime.

MEG *hands* LOU *the paper.* LOU *reads.*

LOU. 'I believe the bicentenary offers us not only a chance to say how profoundly shameful the slave trade was – how we condemn its existence utterly and praise those who fought for its abolition, but also to express our deep sorrow that it could ever have happened and rejoice at the better times we live in.'

MEG. This is all mixed up.

LOU. I know, right? He's trying to say that it wasn't a crime against humanity, that it was normal thinking in those days.

MEG. How could it be normal if we all knew it was wrong? Master Carpenter mutilated my boy and got away with it. Because he paid money for me at auction he thought he owned me. Thought everything I owned was his too, but the child was mine, a sacred secret deep inside me. I knew he would take it away and sell it if he found out, so I hid my

belly from him. And then I concluded that it would be better
to kill the child than for it to be given over to him. When it
was born I stuffed the baby's mouth with rags to quiet it.
I put a cloth over its face and held its nose until it became
a loose limp thing. I dug a hole with my bare hands and
buried it, gently piling earth like a loving mother putting her
baby to bed. Days later people said they heard a baby crying
in the night, said it was a ghost until they traced its cries to
where I'd buried it. When they dug it up the child was still
alive. Master Carpenter said what I had done was a crime,
and that I would be punished. He made me watch as he...
I had to watch as he...

LOU (*gentle*). Don't... Not if it distresses you.

MEG. It is my story.

LOU. And I want to hear it.

MEG. They-they-they they... mmmmm... they... mmmm...
they cut-cut out his tongue. Mmmmmmmm... mmmmmmmm...

LOU. That's... that's... I'm sorry. I'm so so sorry.

MEG. They said I must keep the baby because it would remind
me of what I had tried to do... Enough now, Meg. Time to
forget. Do you want me teach you the quadrille?

LOU. I can take it. Speak, Meg.

MEG. Carpenter brought me here to England with him, to work
with him and to serve him. He was a man of furies. I told
myself that I would not die by his hand. When he raised his
hand to me I turned that whip hand against him and now
I am the fury. The fury is a passion in my legs. I ran. I have
been running ever since. (*Slight pause.*) You understand,
don't you?

LOU. Yes-yes. The fury is a passion in my legs.

MEG (*to* LOU). Your man Blair says that you live in better
times. If this is true then it is indeed cause for rejoicing. Tell
me: Is it true? Do you live in better times? Are you free?

LOU....

Scene Thirteen

1840. A public house in London. The ball of blacks. A small band of musicians plays a waltz. A few couples dance together. LUCY *enters with* MEG *and* JESS *who wears the patchwork ballgown.*

JESS. Oh, look at them all. They all look very fine.

LUCY. And so do you. You're the prettiest girl here.

A BOY *approaches* JESS *and indicates that he would like to dance.*

He's asking you to dance. Go to it.

JESS. I don't want to.

LUCY. No one will see your pretty dress if you hang back here with an old woman like me.

There is a change of tune. JESS *takes up the offer, executes a little curtsy and is off reeling with him.* LUCY *watches proudly.*

2007. LOU's *home.* REUBEN *enters carrying a wine glass. He has a bag on his shoulder.*

REUBEN. What are you doing hiding in here? You should be entertaining your guests.

LOU. Just looking at the river.

REUBEN. It's a beautiful night. (*Slight pause.*) Do you wish you'd gone to the ceremony?

LOU *shakes her head.*

LOU. I wanted to look at the painting.

REUBEN. You'll give yourself nightmares. Want some?

LOU *nods.* REUBEN *feeds her his wine. They embrace and slow dance.*

(*Singing along to a song we can't hear.*) 'And I hope that you feel the same way too…'

LOU. You sentimental idiot.

BENJAMIN *comes out of the crowd.*

LUCY. A ball of blacks. Whatever next?

BENJAMIN. You ask me it's about time.

LUCY. You've cleaned up nice. Begging obviously pays.

BENJAMIN. Me and the boys is cleaning up on the guilt of the abolitionists.

LUCY. You'd better make the most of it, there's no knowing how long it's going to last.

BENJAMIN. My brother still at sea?

LUCY. There's a need in him. I couldn't stop him.

BENJAMIN. If you were mine I'd never leave you.

LUCY. Well, I'm not yours, am I? I'm not anybody's. I'm free.

BENJAMIN. I'll drink to that – (*Offers his arm.*) May I?

LUCY. Oh, I'm not one for dancing, Benjamin.

BENJAMIN. Go on, Luce. Even you must enjoy yourself some time. Today of all days. As my brother isn't here today I'll take his role and ensure that you are happy.

REUBEN. I don't want to go. I'd rather stay here with you than dig around in those old archives.

LOU. You'll be back before you know it. It's very important that you dig around in those old archives.

REUBEN. When I come back I'll teach you to dive. We'll swim in this river.

LOU. We can if you want to catch some horrible disease.

LUCY. I'm tired, Jess. I'm off home.

JESS. And leave me alone?

LUCY. They're all friends here.

JESS. Be happy, Mamma. When do we ever get to enjoy ourselves?

BENJAMIN. You can't go. This is our ball.

REUBEN. I've got a present for you.

REUBEN *reaches into his bag and takes out a lump of metal.*

Guess what that is.

LOU *shrugs.*

It's from that shipwreck *The Glory* that we discovered off the coast of Turks and Caicos.

REUBEN *hands* LOU *the object. She holds it as though it is sacred.*

I know, right?

JESS *is approached by the young man. She goes off to dance.*

BENJAMIN. I know why you don't dance. I know the memories that torment you, but this is a dance for ourselves, There is no ship's captain here, flogging you to jig aboard a deck slippery with the blood of another dancer. Dancing pertains to a freedom of the body. God's life force given to us in music and movement. Celebrate that, at least.

LUCY. I don't know these dances.

BENJAMIN *takes* LUCY*'s hand and pulls her onto the floor, showing her the dance, she follows his steps.*

REUBEN. Slave ships lost weight because the captives would die or commit suicide. This ballast compensated for those losses, holding the weight of the ship. Even if the bodies of the captives remained on board the slavers still needed a counterweight.

MEG *enters. She seems afraid to approach, but goes to it. She wanders through the crowd, finds* LUCY *and* BENJAMIN *and steps between them. She takes* LUCY *aside.* BENJAMIN *watches at first and then follows them.*

LOU. Because a dead body is lighter than one that's alive. Twenty-one grams. That's what they used to say was the difference between a living and dead body, isn't it? Twenty-one grams is the weight of the soul that leaves the body.

LUCY. Meg, you came. Well, this is something to celebrate.

MEG (*African accent*). I was in two minds, Mistress Lucy. I didn't know if to come and find you here or wait for you to come home. If I wait I think how you will be happy, and drunk maybe, so I decided to come now.

LUCY. Slow down, Meg.

MEG. It's the curse, Miss Lucy. Everything I touch catches fire and turns to ashes.

LUCY. Stop that now. No more…

MEG. I tell you I burn, Miss Lucy. I shouldn't have stayed with you so long. I knew it would end badly sooner or later, that you would all burn too. Something bad has happened.

LUCY. What's happened to you, Meg?

REUBEN. We know that this ship started as a slaver, but after emancipation became a merchant vessel. The records show that she made several simple trade voyages up to the date of her wreckage.

LOU. And yet you found ballast on her. It continued to trade even after emancipation.

MEG. Two men called at the house, said they'd something important news for you.

LOU. I'd better get back to the party.

LUCY. Who was it, Meg? What did they tell you?

MEG. They was sailors, Lucy. With news from Thomas's ship.

LUCY. So, Thomas is with them? He's come home?

MEG *doesn't reply.* LUCY *reads the tragedy in her face.*

Tell me he's with them, Meg. Say he's come home but too tired to come see me himself.

MEG *shakes her head.*

History seeping through the walls, the pavements, the music we listen to.

REUBEN. Your back is healing.

LUCY. So what? What, Meg?

REUBEN. When we discover a ship we take some of its rotten timber and lay it down on the beach. We lay it down on the beach and we say a prayer. We say a prayer for all those people whose stories have been lost in the sea.

They leave holding hands, passing JESS *who has entered.*

MEG. He's… gone, Mistress Lucy. Thomas is gone.

LUCY. Gone? Gone where?

MEG. He won't be home at all…

LUCY. Tell me where my husband is.

MEG. They took him, Mistress Lucy. The slavers took him.

BENJAMIN. There is no more slavers. Any English ship goes into the Atlantic with slaves will be blasted by the Navy.

MEG. These men, these sailors said the ship left innocent, but when they reached the Cape Coast it revealed itself for what it really is, got fitted out with shackles and chains, and took on living flesh, Thomas and some of the other sailors among them. The Navy found out what they were doing and sent up their rockets and blue lights. Seeing that, the ship made away, casting the captives overboard as they went. Threw them overboard, Lucy. Like they were throwing away waste.

LUCY *breaks down and starts to wail in another language.* JESS *watches on, distraught.*

LUCY. Ifelwa. Ifelwa. Answer me. Ifelwa Ifelwa. Water whisper to me. Tell me where he is. He is not dead. He is not dead. He is not dead.

JESS. What's she saying, Meg? I can't understand her. What language is that?

LUCY *tears her clothes and wails while the frivolities of the ball of blacks continue and get wilder.* MEG *goes to* LUCY. *She puts her hand on* LUCY's *shoulder.* JESS *watches.*

The ball falls away and MEG, LUCY *and* JESS *are left alone.* MEG *hands* JESS *a gourd full of water.* MEG *ululates then* JESS *holds the gourd to* MEG*'s mouth.* MEG *drinks from it and blows the water into* LUCY*'s face in a fine spray. She repeats this several times.* LUCY *kneels on the ground in front of* MEG *who then pours all the water from the gourd onto* LUCY*'s head.* LUCY *ululates, a gut-wrenching howl of grief and defiance.*

Scene Fourteen

2007. Lou's home. LOU *is clearing up after the party.* REUBEN *is asleep on the sofa. A storm outside. A ringing at the bell.* LOU *goes to the door.* ROY *stands there in a raincoat holding an award.*

ROY. Can I come in?

LOU *lets* ROY *in. He takes off his soaking raincoat. Underneath he is dressed as* TURNER.

(*Indicating his costume.*) They had me do a photoshoot after the ceremony. Congratulations.

ROY *gives* LOU *the award. She puts it away.*

I made a nice speech on your behalf. Had people in tears.

LOU. Thanks.

ROY. You should have gone. Especially since you said you would.

LOU. I changed my mind.

ROY. You had a party? An after-the-after-party party?

LOU. Not exactly a party. More of a gathering.

ROY. Funny that, Trevor let it slip – during the after party, which you did not attend – that he was leaving early to attend a party that you'd invited him to. What happened to my invite?

LOU. It wasn't that kind of party.

ROY. Where's my invite, Lou?

LOU. It was just a little get-together.

ROY. Trevor got an invite. He sells you down the Swanee, but you patch it up with him.

LOU. He tried his best, but his hands were tied.

ROY. I've always supported you.

LOU. Look, I'm sorry, but it's late.

ROY. When we were doing *The Tempest* and you got news that you hadn't got that soap, didn't Deanne and I have you over for dinner?

LOU *doesn't reply.*

Did we or did we not have you over for dinner?

LOU. Yes, yes you did. And I appreciate it.

ROY. Didn't you cry on Deanne's shoulder and say she was like a second mother to you? I'm not going to lie. I am hurt. It hurts me to the core that you leave me out like this. I am devastated about what it says about how you see me because I have always had your back.

LOU. Sometimes we need to be on our own. To talk about things without...

ROY. Go on, say it. Without whities like me. / Go on, lump us all in together.

LOU. If you were a friend you'd understand.

ROY. So, aren't you even going to offer me a drink?

LOU. It's all gone.

ROY *picks up a half-drunk glass, pours another half-drunk glass into it.*

ROY. You know me. I'm not fussy. I hope you're not blaming me because your part was cut. I phoned Trevor, I told him you wouldn't be happy. He said the producers were putting pressure on him and that he'd rather make a film than have no film at all. I've never lied to you and I'm not going to now.

I agreed with him. It wasn't just about making a film. This matters to me.

LOU. It's your film. It's always your film.

ROY. I've told you a million times what it was like for me, a working-class lad from the council estate, trying to make it in this industry. I was patronised, given roles of the most stereotypical kind – chirpy cockneys, gangsters.

LOU. It's not the same.

ROY. Why not? Like you, I have a pure pedigree: generations of working-class poor. They were as good as slaves: cheated out of a living wage, flogged or deported for the most trivial crimes.

LOU. They were treated like slaves?

ROY. I believe that, yes. I do not believe that you have a monopoly on suffering.

LOU. If your ancestors wanted to be alleviated of their hardship. All they had to do was save up until they could afford to buy one of mine.

ROY. There were Africans who benefited from the slave trade.

LOU. You're an intelligent man, Roy. Do we really have to go there? Yes, a few Africans profited from the trade, but millions more didn't. I'm too exhausted to have this out with you. Listen, why don't we schedule in one of your nice dinner parties where we can have a drunken debate about slavery versus servitude in the nineteenth century.

ROY. Don't you patronise me, my girl.

LOU. Don't you call me your girl.

ROY. Sorry-sorry. I didn't mean... I meant it like... like a daughter. Which is how I think of you.

Pause.

'No harm.
I have done nothing but in care of thee.
Of thee, my dear one, thee, my daughter, who
Art ignorant of what thou art, nought knowing
Of whence I am, nor that I am more better

Than Prospero, master of a full poor cell,
And thy no greater father.'

LOU.   'More to know
Did never meddle with my thoughts.'

Funny how no one in the audience ever asked how come you
had a birth daughter as dark as me.

ROY. Because it's true, that's why. Anyone can see that you are
your father's daughter.

Slight pause.

It's not my film. It's Turner's. His great painting gave a kick-
start to the movement for abolition when it was beginning to
die a death.

LOU. It shouldn't be his film. It belongs to the enslaved. He
made that painting for them. He painted it for the future to
tell us that it isn't over.

REUBEN *mumbles in his sleep, a muffled snatch of chorus
from the sea shanty we heard earlier.*

ROY. Wonder what he's dreaming about? You, probably.

LOU. Shut up.

ROY. He's sweet on you.

LOU. You think everyone's sweet on me.

ROY. Because they should be.

LOU. My granddad died.

ROY. Why didn't you say? You don't tell me anything these days?

LOU. I wanted that film to speak for the drowned, for those
whose names are lost to us.

ROY. Do you honestly believe that anyone who sees our film
will ever be able to look at his painting in the same way ever
again? And your appearance in it – brief though it is – will
stay with them.

LOU. Turner exhibited another painting that year called *Rockets
and Blue Lights*. It has this tremendous blue sky in it. I imagine

he found consolation in that blue sky after working on *Slavers*.
He had to cleanse himself from the darkness of his vision.

ROY. You need blue skies too. Let yourself off the hook.

> 'Wipe thou thine eyes; have comfort.
> The direful spectacle of the wreck, which touch'd
> The very virtue of compassion in thee,
> I have with such provision in mine art
> So safely ordered that there is no soul –
> No, not so much perdition as an hair
> Betid to any creature in the vessel
> Which thou heard'st cry, which thou saw'st sink.'

LOU. If only... Wave a magic wand and we could all live
happily ever after. You should have spoken up for me. You
saw what they were doing. You saw them squeezing me out.
And you let them do it.

ROY. I waited my whole life for a part like this. And when it
came I couldn't let it slip away. I am not as powerful as you
think. My old man... his life was... I had to watch him... I'll
make it up to you. Tell me how I can make it up to you.

LOU. Do better, Roy. Educate yourself.

The doorbell.

ROY. Want me to get it?

LOU. I'll go.

LOU *opens the door.* ESSIE *stands in the doorway,
soaking wet.*

LOU *lets* ESSIE *in.*

You. From the exhibition. You decided to come after all. It's
nice to see you, but you're too late. It's all over.

ESSIE *just stands there.*

Come in. You're soaking wet.

ESSIE. Water's not clear like in your film. It's murky and
poisonous. It fills your nose and ears and mouth like smoke.
I dived in. I swam in the dark, searching for him, opened my
eyes over and over, but I couldn't see anything but the black

water. Dive down deeper, feel for him. Even with the river on fire it didn't light up the depths below. He's down there somewhere but they can't find him.

LOU. Who's down there?

ESSIE. Billie.

ROY. Who's Billie?

LOU. He fell in the river?

ESSIE. The boat caught on fire. All that wood. The flames raced across the deck so quickly. They got us all off then someone saw a boy clinging to the mast. He climbed higher and higher chased by the flames that ate the mast till its embers plunged into the water. Sparks flew up to the sky and at first I thought it was Billie flying, but it couldn't have been, could it? Dive in. Swim for Billie, feel for him. Nothing but the dark water, filling my ears, my nose, my mouth like smoke.

Scene Fifteen

A storm at sea. TURNER *is in nightdress standing on what is left of a shipwreck. He holds onto a naked mast, a bottle of gin in one hand, raging at the rumbling sky.*

TURNER. Is that it? Is that all you've got? You can do better than that. Come on, if you think you're hard enough. Is this your mighty retribution? What do you want me to say? Sorry for being such a bad man? For drinking too much gin, and fucking out of wedlock? I do not repent because I have loved every bastard moment. Joseph Mallord William Turner is not ashamed. (*Lightning cracks across the sky, the loud rumble of thunder. He feigns fear.*) Ooh, I'm terrified. I'm quaking in my boots. Call yourself a storm? A toothless old prossie on Hedge Lane could muster more passion than that. Blow wind and crack your fucking cheeks. (*Thunder.*) That's more like it. Again. (*Loud clap of thunder.*) And again and again. Is this how it is to be? Is this how you take your revenge. Mad like Lear's tempest. (*He giggles.*)

There is a knock on the door. All signs of the tempest vanish.

DANBY. You've a guest, Turner. The young man who keeps writing to you.

TURNER. At this time of the night? Send them away.

DANBY. It's midday. It's that boy, Ruskin.

TURNER gets himself together, puts the gin away. He opens the door. RUSKIN enters.

RUSKIN. Here you are, the great man.

TURNER (*looking about*). Where? Where is he, this fellow?

You mocking me?

DANBY. He's no harm. Can't you see that he adores you?

TURNER. Yes, yes I see it.

RUSKIN. If I may, I have a question about the painting: It is called '*Slavers Throwing Overboard the Sick and the Dying – Typhoon Coming On.*' The painting does not depict the slavers nor the action that the title describes. Why is that?

TURNER. You have to work that out for yourself. I only do the painting.

DANBY. Were we to see the falling bodies, the intensity of our horror would exonerate us from all blame and involvement. The act is done, so it is incumbent on us to contemplate the consequences.

DANBY goes.

RUSKIN. Do they hurt you, the critics?

TURNER. Nah. (*Slight pause.*) How old are you?

RUSKIN. Twenty-one.

TURNER. When you are sixty-five, when you smell death's filthy breath, then you won't give a shit what they say about you.

RUSKIN. How do you do it?

TURNER. Now you're asking.

RUSKIN. How does one capture the sublime?

TURNER. You think my *Slave Ship* sublime?

RUSKIN. Yes.

TURNER. If you'll excuse me I've work to do.

RUSKIN. Did I say something wrong?

TURNER. You said everything right. You praised me just the right amount, asked questions… You've nothing to feel embarrassed about. Griffith sent your review… You are very kind.

RUSKIN. My words can't match the…

TURNER (*holds up his hand*). I've work to do.

RUSKIN. I thank you for your time. I am honoured to know you.

TURNER. And I you.

RUSKIN *stares at* TURNER, *star-struck*.

Sometimes I see a painting in a dream. Or I appear in the dream myself. And I am all things in it. I am the slave ship. Wrecked. Empty. I am a shark: The speed of me through water. Livid with the desire for blood. I am the sea boiling with fury. A terrified enslaved woman screams in my arms, her fear pulsing against my chest. She slips through my fingers like water and I am drenched as she plunges into the ocean. Disappears and I can't get her back.

RUSKIN. Yes. Yes, I see.

TURNER. Come see me again, young Ruskin.

RUSKIN. I will. Yes, I will.

RUSKIN *goes.* TURNER *notices a circle of light on the floor. He opens a trap door and pulls back repulsed at the stench from below. The sound of groans and pained suffering.*

TURNER (*calling*). Thomas. You down there? Thomas.

He falls back as he sees something. A hand emerges,
followed by BILLIE *who pulls himself out and stands,*
looking down at TURNER.

Scene Sixteen

The docks. The Glory. JESS *and* LUCY *are with* DECKER *who*
is restless.

DECKER (*indicates the ship*). *The Glory* will look after you.
The sea changes moment to moment, much as the world
changes, but this ship will not change. Oh, she's had several
names, been through several different transformations, but
she remains constant in this: she merges the worlds of earth
and water. I would remain at sea forever if I could.

JESS. I am a shantyman. My mother here is a cook.

DECKER. A shantyman, eh? Well, let's hear yer.

JESS takes out a harmonica and strikes up a tune. JESS
sings 'Our Ship She Lies in Harbour'.

Sometimes at sea you'll be hit by a tempest and you tell
yourself that every bad thing you've ever done in your
lifetime is now being visited upon you. You had thought that
Neptune would turn a blind eye, but a storm tells you that
nature will not let you get away with it. The sea lashes you
so hard it leaves stripes on your back and once I was struck
by lightning, made me blind for moment. This will be my
last voyage. I long for the forgetfulness of old age because
I long to to forget all that I have seen and done.

LUCY (*African*). Tell him that we are not interested in his
distress. Tell him that we do not want him to forget. Tell him
that we need him to remember.

JESS. She lost a husband to the sea and I a father. She thinks
this voyage will bring him back to her, but I know different.
He is lost forever. We make this journey for ourselves now.
We seek a new life.

LUCY (*African*). Where is the ship?

DECKER. What's she say?

JESS. She is impatient to board. She longs for Africa.

DECKER. You'll see such beauty. When the ship rounds the Cape, that first sight of it is like heaven on Earth. You'll see creatures never seen before, like foretold in myths.

JESS. This is all we ask for, mister.

LUCY (*African*). Thomas said the sea would bring his words to us, but I can't hear anything.

DECKER. You'll both take articles. You'll bring us comfort on our voyage. (*He produces the papers from his back pocket.*) Your mark here and here.

LUCY *and* JESS *make their marks on the articles.*

There, you have signed your lives into the care of King Neptune. He'll not fail you. Follow his rules and he'll not let you down.

JESS *strikes up another shanty, sings:*

JESS. See to it that you make your way
    Through the storms that may rise today
    Promise to obey the wind
    For my love lies there within

LUCY. She tells her secrets to the waves and listens as they answer. What do they say, Jess? Do you understand the language of the sea? I'll teach you. I've been neglectful lately. I should have taught you how to swim by now. Look-look, Jess. Can you see? Out there in the distance they're sending up more rockets. Imagine, Jess, that is the last thing Thomas would have seen. Have you ever seen anything so beautiful? There it is: An explosion of blue light, the bluest blue you've ever seen in your life. A sudden intervention on this dark, dark sea. A vista of blue, the sky descending to engulf us like we are walking in the heavens.

JESS *continues to sing.*

Scene Seventeen

A plantation in Brazil. THOMAS *works cutting cane, an* OVERSEER *watches him, rifle pointed at* THOMAS. *As he cuts* THOMAS *sings.*

THOMAS. See to it that you make your way
    Through the storms that may rise today
    Promise to obey the wind
    For my love lies there within

OVERSEER (*Portuguese*). *Cala a boca!* [Shut up!]

    THOMAS *continues to sing.* OVERSEER *shakes his rifle.*

THOMAS. Songs do have a power about them, don't they?

I've seen sailors mutiny to the rhythm of a shanty. Yes, songs are dangerous.

    THOMAS *continues his song. The* OVERSEER *cocks his rifle.* THOMAS *stops singing.*

Memories survive the centuries. There's some say you should forget about where you come from because to remember is to open deep wounds, but I hold my memories close to, for they remind me that I am a man. I've a daughter and wife. Beauties both. They'll think me dead… disappeared into the sea by now.

Works.

I'm not surprised by your fear of me. After all, I have survived much. I survived the slave castles at Bonny, the *Zong* and Baptist massacres. I was there. Witnessed all. Survived it. I survived the fires of New Cross and Grenfell; Death in custody, through all this I lived.

OVERSEER. *Cala a boca.*

    OVERSEER *cocks gun.*

    THOMAS *works.*

THOMAS. I am Yaa Asantewaa, Yvonne Ruddock, David Oluwale.

    As THOMAS *recites these names they are picked up in a chorus by members of the cast, overlapping each other to create a brief echoing effect as though conjuring ghosts.*

I am Sam Sharpe, Kelso Cochrane, Stephen Lawrence. Pull your trigger. I am not afraid of death. I have lived and died ten million times. And I will live and live again.

OVERSEER, *trembling, points gun at* THOMAS *who has stopped working. Play ends.*